How to Find Your Gratitude Attitude

A 21-day Devotional

Also by Aminata Coote

Through God's Eyes: Marriage Lessons for Women

How to Find Your Gratitude Attitude

A 21-day Devotional

Aminata Coote

Names: Coote, Aminata | How to Find Your Gratitude Attitude
Subjects: Problem-Solving—Religious aspects--Christianity
Identifiers: B079XSQ76Y | 978-1980341406 (pbk.)

Cover design by Aminata Coote
Image courtesy of Canva.com

Acknowledgements

I want to thank the Coote men for giving me privacy to write and also for being my beta-listeners. Your attention and comments helped to create this book. Thank you for always believing and encouraging me to follow my dream. I love you both (equally but in different ways).

Denise, Shantel, Kaysia—my beta-readers. Ladies, thank you for taking the time to read and offer feedback. I appreciate your friendships because when I thought about asking someone to read my first draft, I just knew that you were the ones I wanted to be the first readers.

Table of Contents

Table of Contents

Introduction

How to Find Your Gratitude Attitude is a 21-day devotional structured to allow you to look at the unique situations in your life with the aim of helping you to change your perspective. There are many things which happen in our lives that cause us to feel neglected or hurt—sometimes these things are out of our control.

We can't control how our employers or family members treat us. We can't control the economic condition of the country we live in. We can't control each and every situation in our lives.

What we can control is how we react to them. Are we going to be petulant and ungrateful? Or, are we going to find our gratitude attitude and be thankful for the positive which can be found in even the most trying of circumstances?

My prayer for you, for us, is that as we work through this devotional we will take some time to honestly evaluate our lives and the attitude we approach it with.

Are you being grateful and acknowledging God's hand in your life? If not, what's preventing you from doing so?

Feel free to make this book your own—highlight key points, scribble in the margins, grab a notebook or a journal, answer the questions, and get involved).

The most important thing I can urge you to do is to prayerfully engage with the Scripture—read the daily verse in your Bible, underline it, make notes of your observations.

Take it a step further and read the additional Scripture passage each day. Reading the Bible can change your life and will be the key to helping you find your gratitude attitude.

Love,
Ami

Day 1: What Are You Complaining About?

On the next day all the congregation of the children of Israel complained against Moses and Aaron, saying, "You have killed the people of the LORD." Numbers 11:41 NKJV

I know, it's ironic to start a book on gratitude with a verse about complaining, but I wanted to be real. I complain a lot. I complain about my finances and the way every pay period finds me a *little* bit short. I complain about the number on the scale when I step on it. I complain about the way my hair looks when I comb it. Am I alone in the pity party?

My friend, do you find yourself complaining a little more than you should? Let's work on our perspective together. Instead of complaining about the few things I lack, I'm choosing to be grateful all the bills are paid, there's food in the house, there are treats to keep us sweet and I have hair to comb.

Your turn:

What do you find yourself complaining about?

Find your gratitude attitude. Rewrite your statements above.

Pray:

Lord, sometimes I find myself focusing on the things I lack, give me new eyes to see the bounty you have provided. Create in me a heart of gratitude and a tongue that praises instead of complains. In Jesus' name. Amen.

Further reading: Numbers 16:41–50

How would you respond if God showed up at a time when you were complaining?

Did you notice that the people accused Moses of "killing the people of God" and then 14 700 died in the plaque? Are we speaking negativity in our lives? Be honest, what negative things have you spoken over your life?

Seek God's forgiveness. Replace those negative thoughts with positive ones.

Day 2: Window-Shopping Can Lead to Envy

When I saw among the spoils a goodly Babylonish garment, and two hundred shekels of silver, and a wedge of gold of fifty shekels weight, then I coveted them, and took them; and, behold, they are hid in the earth in the midst of my tent, and the silver under it. Joshua 7:21 KJV

Are we living on the spoils of the world? I get it, I really do—it seems sometimes as though everyone is doing better than you are. Your friend's marriage seems happier than yours. The singles in your life seem to have "more fun". Your neighbour's house is bigger or their car is prettier or—whatever!

This window shopping into another person's life gets so much worse when we plug into social media. Everyone's picture makes their lives look so polished and complete and you wonder, "What happened to me? Why can't I look elegant and sophisticated? Why can't I have what they have?"

My darling friend, don't fall into the trap of comparison and envy. Not everything that *looks* pretty is worth having. It's especially not worth having if God doesn't *choose* it for you.

What are you coveting from someone else's life?

List the possible reasons that God doesn't want you to have it (whatever "it" is for you) in this season of your life.

Pray:

Abba Father, sometimes I get drawn in by the lust of my eyes—I see something and tell myself I should have that. Help me not to window shop in other people's lives. Teach me instead how to appreciate the things I do have. In Jesus' name. Amen.

Further reading: Joshua 7:13–22, Genesis 3:1–6

What parallels do you see between the fall in Eden and the sin of Achan?

What lessons can you apply to your own life?

Day 3: Why Does the Wicked Prosper & Righteous Suffer?

The LORD asked, "Is it right for you to be angry?" HCSB
Jonah 4:4

I know the feeling: you try your very best to serve God. You study your Bible. You spend hours in prayer, attend church and do everything you can to live by his commands... But still, sometimes it seems as if you can't get a break. On the other hand, your coworker, or neighbor or family member or friends who live in open rebellion against God seem to be prospering in ways you aren't.

You remember Psalm 73 written by Asaph and try to convince yourself that the wicked prosper only for a time. Nonetheless, at the back of your mind there's this niggling suspicion that this person's blessings are actually coming from God.

"Why God?" you ask, "Why are you blessing _____ and not me?" You may even find yourself getting angry at God. "It's not fair." you may tell him. "Bless me as well."

If we are not careful, the attitude above can fill our hearts with resentment and cost us our relationship with God. We don't know how God's mind works, but in cases like this we just have to remind ourselves that he wants all of us to be saved. He doesn't want any single person to perish.

We have to reach for our gratitude attitude and thank God for the things he is doing in our lives instead of wishing bad for our neighbors. We need to also remind ourselves that salvation comes from God through our belief in and acceptance of the sacrifice of Jesus Christ. None of us *deserve* to be saved because our actions cannot wash away our sins.

Instead of getting mad about that person's success, let's take it as an opportunity to thank God for the things he is doing in their lives. We should also pray for their conversion; pray they will repent of their sins and accept their place in the family of God.

Who is that person in your life who seems to be flourishing outside of a relationship with God? Write a prayer that God will reveal himself to them and that they will acknowledge him as Lord and Savior.

Pray:

Jehovah, forgive me for getting mad when you choose to bless others. Help me instead to find opportunities to glorify your name when I see you working in the lives of the people around me. Remove the scales from their eyes so they are able to see you and enter into a saving relationship with you. In Jesus' name. Amen.

Further reading: Jonah 3:10–4:1–11

Why did Jonah get angry with God?

What was the lesson God was trying to teach Jonah with the plant?

How might you apply that lesson to your own life?

17

Day 4: Complacency Can Lead to Ingratitude

The descendants of Joseph responded, "It's true that the hill country is not large enough for us. But all the Canaanites in the lowlands have iron chariots, both those in Beth-shan and its surrounding settlements and those in the valley of Jezreel. They are too strong for us." Joshua 17:16 NLT

Living complacent is something we do very well as children of God. We get to a place where things become familiar and we settle in. Even when the writing on the wall is telling us to move on. I remember praying for God to remove me from a particular job. Nine years later, I was still there. Yes I had sent out applications but I hadn't *pursued* anything. I remained because I am comfortable.

Is that you? Have you settled into your situation to the point where you start believing this is all God wants for you? Are you living on a plateau when God wants you to conquer the mountain?

In today's key verse, the descendants of Joseph had been allotted a plot of land. All they had to do was drive out the Canaanites and occupy their territory. It

18

would have been a difficult task, but it wasn't impossible. God had already given them the land and had promised to be with them.

They had defeated many nations greater than themselves which should have given them courage. Instead, they doubted. In their minds, the enemy they faced was greater than the God they served and so they settled—squatting on a tiny portion of a land that was actually theirs.

Have you stayed in a situation long past the time God had intended for you to be there?

Make a list of those things you're settling for.

Personalize Deuteronomy 28:13, write it in your notebook/journal and put your name in it.

What are those things God has commanded you to do that you are struggling to obey?

Pray:

Lord, I'm thankful for the territory you have given me. Help me to claim my full inheritance and those blessings you have set aside for me. In Jesus' name. Amen.

Further reading: Deuteronomy 28:5–8

What promises of the Lord are you claiming today?

Day 5: Loneliness Can Lead to Ingratitude

Where shall I go from your Spirit? Or where shall I flee from your presence? Psalm 139:7 ESV

L et's face it: we live in a world where loneliness is fostered. We are encouraged to be social with people all over the world at the cost of ignoring those who live in our communities, on our streets and in our homes. The internet makes it so easy to "connect" with others that sometimes we don't realize we're starved for attention and love.

I know you're wondering: what does loneliness have to do with gratitude? Have you ever felt lonely? Have you noticed that if left unchecked, loneliness can lead to thoughts of hopelessness which eventually leads to depression?

Then the next thing you know you're curled up into a ball wailing about all the things you don't have completely ignoring the bounty at your fingertips.

Okay, so maybe that's a little dramatic. However, if we are not careful, focusing on our loneliness can rob us of our gratitude attitude. Here's what I want us to remember: **being alone doesn't mean we have to be lonely.**

Being alone means we have the perfect opportunity to spend some time with God who loves us like no one on earth can. God loves us enough to be with us at all times.

When the feelings of loneliness creep in, this is when we should remind ourselves there is nowhere that we can go from the presence of God.

Do you remember a time when you felt lonely to the point of despair? Make note of that time in your journal.

Looking back, can you identify the signs that God remained with you throughout the experience?

Pray:

O Great Yahweh, it is so awesome to know that you, the Creator of heaven and earth, care so much about me you are always with me—even when I don't acknowledge your presence. Forgive me for my selfishness in choosing the friendships of the world instead of an abiding relationship with you. Help me to get better at choosing you each day. In Jesus' name. Amen.

Further reading: Psalm 139:7–12

How do the words of the psalmist make you feel about God? Make a note in your journal. .

Make a plan of action for the next time you feel loneliness creeping in. How will you remain grateful?

Day 6: Be Grateful for the Bounty

"Am I supposed to take my bread, my water, and my meat that I butchered for my shearers and give them to these men? I don't know where they are from." I Samuel 25:11 HCSB

There was a man named Nabal. He had 3 000 sheep and 1 000 goats. During the time of the sheep shearing, David sent a request to him for food. Now, it was the custom during that time for the food prepared during the harvest to be shared with others. Instead of reaching out in kindness or obedience, Nabal chose to be unkind. He chose ingratitude.

God gives us, not only to meet our needs; he gives us so we will have something to share with others. Are you living life as though you have nothing to offer your neighbor?

Take an inventory of your life: what do you have an abundance of?

Make a plan to share some of your excess.

Pray:

Jehovah, forgive me. I forget to give you thanks for all the things I do have focusing instead on what I don't. Help me to be a helping hand to those around me. In Jesus' name. Amen.

Further reading: I Samuel 25:2–11

Make a list of all the things Nabal had to be grateful for.

Make a list of all the things you have to be grateful for.

Write a prayer to thank God for them.

Day 7: When We Forget to Be Grateful

"What did they see in your palace?" Isaiah asked. "They saw everything," Hezekiah replied. "I showed them everything I own—all my royal treasures." II Kings 20:15 NLT

This verse bothers me. Here is a king who had just been saved from death (literally!). Hezekiah had been on his death bed when he prayed to God for a miracle. God heard his prayer and gave him an additional fifteen years to live. God also displayed his awesomeness by causing the sun to go back ten degrees.

Hezekiah had two miracles happen in a very short span of time yet, when the ambassadors from Babylon came to inquire about his health, all he could boast about were his possessions.

Are we forgetting how to be grateful? Write down three things God has done that you forgot to give him thanks for.

Write your prayer of thanksgiving.

Make a plan of action to share future blessings with others.

Pray:

Jehovah I am sometimes shortsighted. I can't see clearly the blessings you have placed in my life. Open my eyes that I may see the wondrous things you are doing in my life and in the lives of those around me. Give me a heart of gratitude and let praise for you to flow from my lips. In Jesus' name. Amen.

Further reading: II Kings 20:1–11

What could Hezekiah have said to the ambassadors instead of showing them his treasury?

What were some of the consequences of his boastful pride?

How can you apply those lessons to your own life?

27

Day 8: Who Are We to Question God?

"Who is this that darkens counsel by words without knowledge? Dress for action like a man; I will question you, and you make it known to me. "Where were you when I laid the foundation of the earth? Tell me, if you have understanding. Job 38:1–3 ESV

The truth is: God doesn't owe us any explanations. He's not obligated to provide us with rain, sunshine, good health or any of the things he lavishes on us. Yet, we continue to demand and expect things that really don't belong to us.

When we remember God is our father and we are his children, it puts a lot of our conversations in perspective. In fact, those of us who are parents would accuse any child of ours who spoke to us in the manner we sometimes speak to God as being ungrateful. Why then do we speak to the Sovereign Lord as though he were here to grant our every desire?

We ask and ask and get sulky when our demands are not met. It is only because God is so gracious that he allows us to continue to speak to him the way we do.

What are some of the attitudes that you display towards God which you would find undesirable in your children?

If the positions were reversed (God was the child and you were his parent), how would you respond to the attitudes mentioned above?

Pray:

Lord, forgive me for not acknowledging your place as Adonai. I ask that you will help me to be grateful for all the blessings you have given so freely to me. I no longer want to behave as a petulant child. Teach me instead to be gracious. In Jesus' name I pray. Amen.

Further reading: Psalm 103

Which of the blessings listed in this psalm are you most grateful for?

Write a psalm with a similar theme mentioning specifically those things God has done for you.

How might this help you to find your gratitude attitude?

Day 9: Should the Creation Question the Creator?

But who are you, O man, to answer back to God? Will what is molded say to its molder, "Why have you made me like this?" Has the potter no right over the clay, to make out of the same lump one vessel for honorable use and another for dishonorable use?" Romans 9:20–21 ESV

There are times when I wish I had been born with the skinny gene. My husband wishes he had been born without it. Each of us has reasons for wanting to wish away an integral part of who we are, yet none of us has the right to demand it. Is that you my sweet friend? Are you at a place where you find yourself arguing with God?

"Abba, why did you make my thighs so thick?"

"God, why did you make my hair so kinky?"

"Lord, why did you make me so susceptible to a kind word?"

There are so many questions we can ask God about the way he made us … There's also one very important thing to remember: **God doesn't owe us an explanation.**

Everything he does—including creating us—was done for *his* glory. We are here because God *wanted* us to be here. The very thing we hate about ourselves is the thing he will use to draw others unto himself.

If you could change anything about yourself, what would it be?

Read over your list and think about how God can use those things for his glory. Make a note of them in your journal.

Pray:

Lord, I thank you for making me exactly as I am. Help me to appreciate every aspect of my personality and those things about my body which cannot be changed. Help me to be a blessing to others. In Jesus' name. Amen.

Further reading: Romans 9:14–24

What's the main lesson you learned from this passage about being grateful for how you were made?

Re-read the passage as if God were speaking directly to you; make a note of the verse that most resonates with you.

Day 10: Wishing Away Our Uniqueness

For You formed my inward parts; You covered me in my mother's womb. Psalm 139:13 NKJV

Have you ever felt unwanted? Unloved? Have you ever wished to be thinner? Prettier? Fairer? Wittier? More intelligent?

There are times when it seems the world is conspiring to make you feel "less than"—as though you don't measure up. Life can hurt your feelings. It can rob you of every shred of self-confidence you have.

If we're not careful, we'll get so used to wishing we were someone else that we spend our whole lives trying to be something we were not created to be. You can easily get to a place where you don't have a clue about who God created you to be because you never took the time to find out.

Is that you my friend? Are you wearing yourself out trying to fit into a mold that was designed in the minds of men? Are you denying parts of your personality as you strive desperately to earn the approval of the people around you?

I have one word for you: stop. Just, stop.

You are not a mistake, or the result of failed contraceptive measures … there was deliberation in your birth. God created you. You are fearfully and wonderfully made and that's a reason to be grateful. Even if no one on earth wants you—God does. You have been specially chosen by him.

Which person on earth is capable of creating life? Aren't you grateful that you were created specifically to be here?

Make a list of all the things that are unique about you.

What items on your list are the results of habits resulting from the influences of the world? What items form part of your unique identity? Re-write your list in two columns: those that can be changed and those that cannot.

Pray:

Jehovah, thank you for creating me and protecting me in my mother's womb. I am grateful you chose to make me and place me in these unique situations here on earth. Thank you for my life. In Jesus' name. Amen.

Further reading: Psalm 139:13–18

Write a letter to God expressing your response to these verses.

Day 11: Blaming God for What's Wrong

Now Martha said to Jesus, "Lord, if you had been here, my brother would not have died. John 11:21NKJV

Maybe those weren't your exact words ... you may have said instead, "Lord if you kept your promises we would have been able to pay the bills." "Lord if you were here, I wouldn't have gotten sick." "Lord, if you had been there, they wouldn't have told lies about me." There are many things that we say to accuse God of abandoning us and we make God into a promise breaker.

"I will never leave you nor forsake you." This was one of God's promises to us yet at times life can feel very lonely. It can feel as though we're all alone in the midst of our troubles. When the pain hits us at 2 o'clock in the morning, we may ask ourselves "Where is God?" When we're facing unemployment or a lack of resources, we may wonder where God is. It's at that point we need to dig deep and find our gratitude attitude.

We have to find the strength to say: "I may be feeling a whole lot of pain but I am grateful for_____."

"The bills are past due but I am thankful _____."

There's always at least one thing to be grateful for, but we may have to dig a little deeper to find it.

Make note of a time when you felt like God had abandoned you.

As you look back on the situation, where do you see his hand?

Pray:

Lord, it is not always easy to believe you are with me in every situation but that's on me. Help me to see you in my every day and in my everything. Help me to trust your heart when it seems as though I can't see your hand.

Further reading: John 11:1–44

Lazarus was dead. How do you think his family was feeling?

What was the reason Jesus had given for not going to him sooner?

What happened when Jesus finally showed up?

What encouragement can you find in this passage?

Day 12: God Is Present in the Struggle

"Pardon me, my lord," Gideon replied, "but if the LORD is with us, why has all this happened to us? Where are all his wonders that our ancestors told us about when they said, 'Did not the LORD bring us up out of Egypt?' But now the LORD has abandoned us and given us into the hand of Midian." Judges 6:13 NIV

Why do we believe that because God is with us we should not have any difficulties? Have we fallen into the trap of believing our lives as followers of Christ should be stress-free and worry-free?

Gideon couldn't understand that though his people were experiencing hardship, God was with them—listening, waiting, hoping for them to turn to him and acknowledge him as Adonai

I'm a lot like Gideon too. At the first sign of trouble, I start questioning God and begging him to help me. But what I really want is for him to make the bad thing go away. Does that happen with you? Do you want God to wrap you in a bubble and protect you from hurt, sadness and pain?

What do you specifically wish God would protect you from?

Why do you think bad things sometimes happen to God's people?

Pray:

Lord, I know you can't always protect me from the consequences of sin. Help me to understand that every experience you allow is an opportunity to draw closer to you. In Jesus' name. Amen.

Further reading: John 16:25–33

What does your brand of tribulation look like?

What kind of hope can you find in Jesus' words in verse 33?

Day 13: Pursued by a Loving God

The LORD has appeared of old to me, saying: "Yes, I have loved you with an everlasting love; therefore with lovingkindness I have drawn you." Jeremiah 31:3 NKJV

My friend, what has God saved you from? Before Jesus stepped in and became the center of your life, what activities were you engaged in? Were you a habitual liar? Did you steal? Was it drugs? Illicit sex? Unbalanced relationships?

Maybe you grew up in the church so rebellion and rabble-rousing were not your thing—perhaps you got lost in the very house of God … can you see how God kept you with him?

Can you look back over the period of your life and trace the hand of God? Can you see how he pursued you? How he loved you? Do you see where the activities you were involved in could have caused your death but he protected you?

Isn't it awesome having the King of the Universe so interested in you he keeps drawing you back to himself? You may have accepted him as your Lord and Savior—and that's absolutely wonderful—but do you see how sometimes you drift away from his presence? Do you see how he loves you endlessly and reminds you he is constantly with you?

God loves you. There is nothing he wants more than to have you spend eternity with him. That thought should have the praises continually on our lips and joy bubbling in our hearts.

What was your life like before you accepted Christ as Adonai?

What evidence do you see of a loving God pursuing you and drawing you back to himself?

Pray:

Abba Father, thank you for loving me. I'm so grateful you did not give up on me. I know I don't always do as I should but I ask that you will continue to pursue me and love me back to yourself. In Jesus' name. Amen.

Further reading: Luke 15:4–7

How do you think the shepherd felt when he realized one of his sheep was missing?

Re-read the passage. Imagine that the shepherd is Jesus and you are the lost sheep. How does it make you feel to know Jesus sought after you until you were restored to the fold?

Day 14: God Has a Plan for Our Lives

"Why did I not perish at birth, and die as I came from the womb? Why were there knees to receive me and breasts that I might be nursed?" Job 3:11–12 NIV

Have you ever wished you were dead? Have you asked God why you were created - not in the sense of "What's my purpose?" but more of an "I think you made a mistake God" kind of way?

I have. It took a long time for me to realize that what I was doing was accusing God of faultiness. When we question our existence, it's like a painting asking the artist why it was created or stating that there is something intrinsically wrong with the design.

Dear friend, I know life is not always easy to bear, but we have to believe that everything in our life happens for a purpose. God did not create us on a whim. We were intricately designed, purposely thought of and placed in a unique set of circumstances to create the you and me who exist today.

God has a plan for your life. It may not be easily seen or understood, but while you're waiting sweet friend, may I suggest that you work on your relationship with God? Take time to study his word and speak with him in prayer. Spend time getting to know him. You'll be glad you did.

What circumstances have you faced that have caused you to question God's plan for your life?

What do you think may have prevented God from giving you an "easy life"?

Pray:

Lord, forgive me for thinking you made a mistake when you created my unique set of circumstances. Help me to remember that you're absolutely perfect and that nothing you do is done carelessly. Help me to seek you with all my heart and all my soul and all my might as I wait to fulfill my purpose. In Jesus' name. Amen.

Further reading: Psalm 139:1–18

What are the things you love about yourself?

Take a moment to thank God for them. Write a prayer which you can revisit the next time you're feeling low.

Day 15: God's Appointment for Us

"I knew you before I formed you in your mother's womb. Before you were born I set you apart and appointed you as my prophet to the nations." Jeremiah 1:5 NLT

L ife can appear to be an endless chain of things that lead nowhere. Growing up, I was taught I needed to do well in school so I could get a good job. If I landed a good job I could afford to buy a house and a car and settle down to produce a family with 2.4 children (not quite sure how to have .4 of a child… but that was the expectation).

I accomplished the first goal: check.

Next, I started working in what I thought were good jobs … but if you're working and do not own a car or a house, does that mean you're not in a "good job"? If you don't have the requisite 2.4 children, are you somehow a failure? If you are not married, does it mean something's wrong with you?

Questions like these can lead to window-shopping and pretty soon you start wondering, "What's the point of all this?"

That's why I love Jeremiah 1:5—it tells me that God has an appointment for me, for you, for each of us, one the world may not agree with. Yet, it is one which would serve to wipe away any thought of ingratitude.

"That verse doesn't apply to me." you're probably thinking, "I'm not a prophet."

Oh yes, you are. We're all prophets.

A prophet is anyone who teaches or proclaims the will of God. Have you told someone about Jesus? You're a prophet. Have you ever explained a passage of Scripture? You're a prophet.

What are Christians if not proclaimers of the will of God? What are people but creations of a holy God called to live a life in loving obedience to El Elyon (God Most High)?

We were all given an assignment. Every single person on earth was given a message, a voice, something to share with those around them. Okay, so you're not a preacher or a Bible study leader, but you have been gifted with culinary skills or hospitality—that's an opportunity to proclaim to others about the will of God.

What unique talents/gifts have you been given by Abba Father? How might they be used to share the good news of salvation with someone?

Make a plan to share your story with someone today.

Pray:

El Elyon, how wonderful to be chosen and given such an awesome responsibility by you. I am grateful to be a part of this great work to share the good news of salvation with the people of this world. Thank you for choosing me as your prophet. I ask for your help as I seek to be an inspiration to those around me. In Jesus' name. Amen.

Further reading: I Corinthians 3:1–11

In this passage, Paul shares with the church at Corinth that there is no need to argue about who led a person to Christ. All persons work together but it is the Holy Spirit that convicts. It is not our action that saves. Only God can save.

Reminisce on your walk with God. How many persons shared with you the love of God which eventually led to you saying yes to him?

If those persons are still alive, take the opportunity to let them know how grateful you are they shared the gospel with you.

How does being considered a "coworker with God" affect your gratitude attitude?

Day 16: Appreciate Answered Prayers

Is this not the word that we told you in Egypt, saying, 'Let us alone that we may serve the Egyptians'? For it would have been better for us to serve the Egyptians than that we should die in the wilderness." Exodus 14:12 NKJV

I watched the building go up with great anticipation. I was unhappy in my present situation and wanted a change. I remember praying, "God, please let the building be finished quickly so I can get a job there."

My prayer was answered and I got a job in the new building but things weren't as good on the inside as they seemed from the outside. "God I hate this job! Please find me a new one." I cried.

Like the children of Israel, I couldn't appreciate the now. Instead, I looked back and idealized my past. Is there something you prayed for that God has blessed you with? You may not be feeling happy about it right now, but remember the fact that God heard and answered your prayer is something to be thankful for.

Make note of a prayer which God answered that you have been complaining about.

Now write a response to yourself (include the reason that prompted the prayer mentioned above).

Pray:

Yahweh, forgive me for my ungratefulness. Help me to cultivate thankfulness. Give me a heart that remembers what you have delivered me from. In Jesus' name. Amen.

Further reading: Exodus 2:23–25

Imagine the Israelites "groaning because of their bondage"; what are some of the things they may have said in their despair?

What are some of the things you have said when you forget to be grateful?

Find your gratitude attitude. Write down three things you have to be thankful for.

Day 17: God's Grace is Sufficient

But he said to me, "My grace is sufficient for you, for my power is made perfect in weakness." Therefore I will boast all the more gladly of my weaknesses, so that the power of Christ may rest upon me. II Corinthians 12:8–9 ESV

When I was fifteen, I woke up one morning and couldn't move. Or I could, but not without excruciating pain. There was so much inflammation in one of my hips I couldn't move it. As the days went by, the pain got less until it eventually went away. That was the beginning of a new life for me—one where joints suddenly stopped functioning without pain and then a few days later, it was as if I had imagined the pain.

Over the years, I have seen a number of doctors and they have drawn dozens of vials of blood trying to figure out the root cause for my pain. I remember praying as I went for the results one day, "Please God, let there be a diagnosis." When I left the doctor's office after the visit with another prescription for more blood tests, I started to feel disappointed. Then, I heard my Father whisper, "My grace is sufficient for you."

Sweet friend, it may be you are suffering from some chronic illness today. Maybe the doctors can't figure out the reason for your ailment or your pain. But my dear, take that as a reason to give thanks to God. You may be wondering, "Why should I tell God thanks for this thing which plagues me?" Because—

Ready for it?

Because God created your unique set of circumstances for you to not only grow closer to him, but to also for you to be a blessing to someone else. It wasn't a mistake. It's not a punishment. It's definitely not a curse, it's a blessing. It's an opportunity for you to share the grace of a loving God with someone who may be struggling in a similar manner.

What difficult set of circumstances have you been struggling with?

How can it be used to be a blessing to someone else?

Pray:

Father God, I know I have been less than gracious about this thorn in the flesh. Today I want to say thank you: thank you Jehovah, for caring enough about me to try to save me and to give me a testimony for others. In Jesus' name. Amen.

Further reading: II Corinthians 1:3–7

How has God comforted you in your distress?

What have you learnt about comforting others from this experience?

Day 18: Rejoice in God's Law

Without prophetic vision people run wild, but blessed are those who follow [God's] teachings. Proverbs 29:18 GW

C an you imagine a world without the law of God? No? Let's imagine it together:

There would be no Jehovah so every man can do as they see fit.

People can create gods from anything, in the likeness of whatever they choose and worship them.

There's no Sabbath rest so our employers can have us work all day long. Every day of the week.

There's no need to show respect to your elders, even if they're your parents.

There are no laws against murder. If a person offends you, it's perfectly okay to do whatever you want to do to them.

It's okay to have sexual relations with anyone because their marital state doesn't matter. That also means anyone can choose to pursue a relationship with *your* partner.

If you see anything and you want it, go for it. There are no boundaries. Take it and do whatever you want with it.

There would be no justice system, but even if there were, it's okay to say someone did something when they didn't.

It's okay to envy what the person beside you has, and if it leads to you taking it, fine. If it means the person loses their life in the process, that's perfectly acceptable.

Now, that sounds a little bit like the world we're living in now, doesn't it? But what if we *all* behaved in this manner? No one would be called to have any standards and so everything was allowed.

Wouldn't that be an even more horrible place to live? Would you want to live in a place like that? Aren't you grateful God has placed his law in the hearts of men? And that some of us still *choose* to follow his standard?

We don't live in a perfect world. However, there remains much to be grateful for.

What conditions do you see in the world that you need to pray about? Make a list of them so that you can add them to your prayer list.

Pray:

Lord, this world is no longer the perfect place you created. I thank you for writing your laws on the hearts of men and that there is still a remnant that chooses to obey your laws. Strengthen the hearts of those who remain faithful to you—may they continue to abide by your word. In Jesus name. Amen.

Further reading: Exodus 20:1–20

How has God's laws impacted your life? Take a moment to say a prayer for their influence on your life.

If you were to teach the Ten Commandments to a child, how would you express them?

Day 19: God's Mercy Is Greater Than Our Failings

Do not remember the rebellious sins of my youth. Remember me in the light of your unfailing love, for you are merciful, O LORD. Psalm 25:7 NLT

Is there anyone reading this who has lived a perfect life? Is there one who made no mistakes and always did as they were told? Is it possible to live without having caused disappointment in the heart of our heavenly Father?

When I was younger I couldn't understand the concept of a God who allowed persons to continually do evil without punishment. It wasn't until I became a parent that I got a little bit of an idea of what happens in the mind of God.

Can you relate? Perhaps your child has done something which defied all the rules and you thought, "Okay. This is it." But then, moments later your heart melts as you realize this is your child, the one you labored to bring into this world.

Or, possibly you did something in your youth which made your parents angry to the point that the only thing left was for them to pack your bags and ask you to leave. Yet, at the end of the day they forgave you and lavished love and attention on you once again.

The mercy and grace displayed here on earth is just an inkling of the abounding love and mercy of the Father. He is totally invested in our care. It is for that reason he keeps trying repeatedly to reach us. He loves us dearly and wants nothing more than to save us from sin.

God's mercy is a reason to be grateful. His unfailing love is to be cherished.

Think about a time in your life when you rebelled against parental rules and received grace. Make a note of that time in your journal:

Write down the evidences of God's unfailing love in your life.

Pray:

El Olam, thank you for the love and mercy that you have displayed in my life. Had it not been for them I would have been destroyed a long time ago. I'm taking this moment to let you know how grateful I am to have been spared. In Jesus' name. Amen.

Further reading: Isaiah 48:12–13 & Exodus 34:6–7

Write down the emotions you experienced as you read the two passages.

How does it make you feel to know that God—this Person with so much power—created you because he wants a relationship with you?

Day 20: Service Reaps a Reward

'Is it not lawful for me to do what I wish with what is my own? Or is your eye envious because I am generous?'
Matthew 20:15 NASB

I love the story of the vineyard owner in Matthew 20. I like to think of the workers as those who would be saved. Each of us was basically standing around looking for something to do with our lives when Christ steps in.

Jesus came and offered us the gift of eternal life. But he didn't stop the search with us—he kept looking and looking until the end of time was near. All the laborers considered themselves equal to the other until it was time for the wages to be paid. Then the master gives everyone the exact same wage and resentment walks in.

The person who worked all day got the same amount as the person who only worked one hour. How unfair is that? Shouldn't the ones who did more work get a higher wage?

It's easy to complain until we realize that's how it will be when Jesus returns for us. The person who served him all their life will get the same reward as someone who met him ten seconds before their death.

Isn't that much fairer? Aren't you happier knowing each of us will reap the same reward for our service? No? Think about it this way: there are many mansions in heaven and those who are faithful will receive one. But the bigger your mansion, the more successful a Christian you were thought to be by God. How would that be different than what happens here on earth?

Imagine a heaven and a New Jerusalem with the same system of reward that earth does, would you want to spend eternity there?

How would you feel if the mansions in heaven had varying sizes and different levels of beautification dependent on your 'Christianity meter'?

Pray:

Yahweh, I'm so thankful you treat all your children the same. There are times when I don't understand that and wish things were otherwise—help me to learn to love others as you love them. Create in me a loving heart. In Jesus' name. Amen.

Further reading: Matthew 20:1–15

Imagine yourself as the laborer who began working in the morning. How would you feel at pay time when you see the person who worked one hour receive the same wage you did?

Read Matthew 20:1–15 again. This time imagine yourself as the person who only worked one hour but still got a full days' pay. What would be your attitude? Remember that this story is a parable for the wages paid to all who accept Jesus as Lord and Savior.

Day 21: We Are Complete in Jesus

"and you are complete in Him, who is the head of all principality and power." Colossians 2:10 NKJV

The sad truth of life is that we continually strive to find our identities in all manner of things outside of Yahweh.

I believe there is a missing piece inside of all of us. I call that missing piece the "God-slot". This is what leads us to seek completion. We are always trying to find something which fills the empty space on the inside.

We fill it with food, the pursuit of money, fame and glory. We try to fill it with alcohol and drugs of all kinds.

We pursue relationships hoping to find the one person who will complete us, 'our other half' as we like to say.

But, here's the thing: God designed us so that we would crave a relationship with him. He longs to fill in our missing pieces and make us truly complete.

Nothing can fill our empty places like God can. We are complete in him. Outside of a relationship with Christ, we will continue to be haunted by that missing something.

What have you tried to fill your God-slot with?

How successful were those attempts?

Further reading: Colossians 2:6–10

What are some of the things the apostle notes as being dangerous to our identities in Christ?

What are you susceptible to?

Write Colossians 2:10 in the space below. Get creative. Make it beautiful.

Create a print you can hang somewhere you'll see it every day. Not creative? No problem—download a copy of the free printable from my website at: https://www.hebrews12endurance.com/image-files/i-am-complete-in-jesus.jpg.

Reflection

What was the biggest lesson you learnt over the last three weeks?

Create an action plan to help you find (and keep) your gratitude attitude.

Last Words

Thank you for taking the time to work through this 21-day devotional with me. I hope that you were able to find some things to be grateful for. I implore to keep this devotional and your journal to review whenever you feel that you've lost your gratitude attitude.

I know that it's not always easy to praise God in the midst of your struggles, it's hard to praise when you're in pain … I also know from personal experience that praising God in the midst of those moments make them easier to bear.

On the next page, I'm going to share with you a few prompts to help you when being thankful is the last thing you want to do. They are set up as journal prompts. I hope that you'll read them and be encouraged. I pray that you will search God's words for scriptures that cause your heart to brim over with praise so that you can begin your own collection.

Also included are blank pages for you to complete days 22 to 28. This was done intentionally to give you an opportunity to write your own gratitude attitude journal. Drop me a line at Aminata@hebrews12endurance.com and let me know how you filled those pages.

Now that you've found your gratitude attitude I encourage you to find those verses that inspire you. Write the words that God places on your heart in the spaces along with your experiences or whatever explanation God reveals.

When you pass through the waters, I will be with you; and when you pass through the rivers, they will not sweep over you. When you walk through the fire, you will not be burned; the flames will not set you ablaze. Isaiah 43:2 NKJV

How does this verse encourage you to remain grateful?

God is our refuge and strength, a very present help in trouble. Psalm 46:1 ESV

Make a list of the ways you God has been your refuge. Include those times when he 'showed up' when you least expected it.

In your journal, write the lyrics to a song that helps you find your gratitude attitude.

Write other verses that can serve as "gratitude attitude" reminders.

Day 22

Day 23

Day 24

Day 25

Day 26

Day 27

Day 28

About the Author

Aminata Coote is a wife, mother, author, and follower of Jesus Christ. She is passionate about helping women to run their race.

Read more from Aminata on her website https://www.hebrews12endurance.com/ where she encourages women to know God, know themselves and run their race.

Connect with Aminata on:

Twitter: @Heb12Endurance

Instagram: @hebrews12endurance/.

Facebook: www.facebook.com/Hebrews12Endurance/

ALSO AVAILABLE

FROM AMINATA COOTE

What do we really know about marriage? Is it just about the happily ever after?

We find Mr. Right, a nice venue, a ring, a beautiful dress and a pair of tux. We promise "till death do us part". If it's that simple, why do so many marriages end in divorce? Could it be that we're looking at marriage from the wrong perspective?

Through God's Eyes: Marriage Lessons for Women is a Bible study that invites you to:

- Look at your marriage through the lens of the Bible.
- Learn from the ancients how to have the marriage God intends.
- Embrace your role as a wife as you draw closer to your Heavenly Father.

Study the biblical couples and learn what God intended (and did not intend) for marriage.

Made in the USA
Columbia, SC
29 June 2021